DIVORCE:
Through the Eyes of God's Love

JOHN ALLEN JR.

ISBN 978-1-63525-348-1 (Paperback)
ISBN 978-1-63525-349-8 (Digital)

Copyright © 2016 by John Allen Jr.
All rights reserved. No part of this publication may be reproduced, distributed, or transmitted in any form or by any means, including photocopying, recording, or other electronic or mechanical methods without the prior written permission of the publisher. For permission requests, solicit the publisher via the address below.

Christian Faith Publishing, Inc.
296 Chestnut Street
Meadville, PA 16335
www.christianfaithpublishing.com

Printed in the United States of America

CONTENTS

Acknowledgments 5
Introduction 7
Chapter 1: What Should I Do Now That I'm Divorced? 9
Chapter 2: Does God Still Love Me? 12
Chapter 3: Will God Forgive Me? 16
Chapter 4: Will God Still Use Me? 22
Chapter 5: What about the Children? 29
Chapter 6: What's Worst? 32
Chapter 7: Can I Remarry? 36
Ordering Information 39
About the Author 40

ACKNOWLEDGMENTS

A very special thanks and all praise, glory, honor, adoration, and admiration be to my God and Father, Jesus my Lord and Savior, and the Holy Spirit, whose temple I am, for calling me, equipping me, anointing me, directing me, and instructing me in the purpose for which I exist—to be God's author.

Avery special thanks goes to my patient supportive, motivating, and loving wife Mrs. Erica Allen. Thanks also goes to my ever encouraging Mother, Bette Reeves, and everyone else who helped in the birth of this book, the first of many.

INTRODUCTION

In this book, we're not focusing on the dos and don'ts of marriage, nor the shoulds and shouldn'ts. God has focused me on the fact that *divorces* are done and finalized and that I should minister to these *divorced* people where they currently are.

May all who read this book be blessed and know that God loves everyone, including *divorced* people.

CHAPTER 1

What Should I Do Now That I'm Divorced?

But seek ye first the kingdom of God, and His righteousness; and all these things shall be added unto you.

—Matthew 6:33

Draw near to God, and He will draw near to you.

—James 4:8a

Wait on the Lord: be of good courage, and he shall strengthen thine heart: wait, I say, on the Lord.

—Psalm 27:14

One of the first things we need to do is ask and accept God's forgiveness for our divorce, whether we believe it's our fault or not. Then, we need to forgive ourselves, which seems to be the area that's preyed on the most, because when you refuse to forgive yourself, *you* open the door for guilt, condemnation, foolish accusations, assumptions, and a host of other things that will hinder your growth with God and yourself. Therefore, it's imperative to forgive yourself and to pursue the act of forgetting, "forgetting those things which are behind and continue to reach or strive forward, always pressing toward the goal that God has for you in Christ Jesus" (Philippians 3:13-14). It's enough to have others holding things against you, reminding you of your divorce at every opportunity they get and attempting to hinder you because of it. You don't need to do it to yourself. Jesus said, "You should love your neighbor as yourself" (Matthew 22:39), which means that in order to love others, you must first love yourself. Likewise, it is with forgiveness; you must first forgive yourself before you can effectively and consistently forgive others. And a word of caution: don't get frustrated and disgusted with yourself if you encounter difficulty forgiving yourself. It takes some people longer to become comfortable with forgiving themselves as well as others because the spirit of your mind has to be renewed and developed in the area of forgiveness.

After you've forgiven yourself and even during your forgiving process, it's time to get as close to God the Father through Jesus Christ as you possibly can. Many people make the mistake of avoiding God during difficult and perplexing times, when God Himself said, "As one whom his mother comforteth, so will I comfort you" (Isaiah 66:13). And Jesus said, "Come unto me all ye that labor and are heavy laden, and I will give you rest" (Matthew 11:28) (emphasis mine). Did you notice in both these verses that God the Father and Jesus the Son welcome and desire to comfort any and all who will allow and accept it; and divorced people are not excluded. So again I say, get as close to God as you possibly can. He can and will comfort you the way you need to be comforted. Drugs will only make things worse. The Holy Spirit, whose temple I am, has enlightened me that many have attempted to lessen the pain of divorce with drugs instead of turning to God, but the drugs have created more problems that they anticipated. Even so, my God says if you return to Him, He will comfort you, deliver you, direct you, lead you, strengthen you, help you, and yes, love you, but you must come to Him. Jesus said, "Come unto *ME.*" (Matthew 11:28) (emphasis mine). Would you please come? Those of you who have tried everything but Jesus, would you come to Him? I promise you, if you come humbly, honestly, and sincerely, you won't be disappointed. I know that many men and women have disappointed you, and many of them were "Christians", but *my Lord Jesus is not a man.* He came as the son of man but he ascended as the Lord of lords, the King of kings, the Captain of our Salvation, the Chief Bishop of our souls, God the Son Himself with all power in His hands. There is no situation or predicament that He can't fix for you. He's able to make any crooked thing straight. But you must take that first step because the Word states, "Draw near to God, and He will draw near to you" (James 4:8a). I am fully persuaded that when you take the first step, God will run to your aid to assist and defend you. He's waiting for you to take that first step, so take it and don't be afraid. Jesus is again saying to you, don't be afraid, be encouraged knowing that He's there for you to help you in any way He can in any way that you will allow Him to help you. And once you've initiated the development of your relationship with Him, never stop developing and strengthening it. Your life will never be the same and always remember, God loves you and so do I.

CHAPTER 2

Does God Still Love Me?

My first response to that question would be an emphatic "Yes!" knowing God the way I do, but we're not just going to accept my answer. We're going to allow God to answer it for Himself.

One of the most familiar passages in the Bible is also one of the most powerful and revealing passages in the Bible relating to God's love and that's John 3:16 which states, "For God so loved the world that He gave His only begotten Son, that whosoever believes in Him should not perish but have everlasting life." Now let us ask you a few questions stemming from this verse. First, when this book was written (Gospel of John), were you born? Scholars have suggested that it was written between 80-120 A.D. because one point is this: If God loved you so much to give His only begotten Son Jesus to die for you before you were even born, why would he cease to love you after you were born? Well, you might say, "I wasn't divorced then." And if you did say or think it that, you missed one of the greatest aspects of God's love, because God's love is omniscient, meaning God knows all things and long before you were born, married and divorced, God loved you. Don't you realize that in eternity past, God knew that you would be divorced? He didn't say, "I'm going to love everybody in the world *except* divorced people." No, John 3:16 said, "For God so loved the world." That's an all-inclusive phrase.

Now our self-righteous church folk and leaders may try to tell you differently as if because they haven't been divorced, they have a monopoly on God's love. What a crock! The truth of the matter is, God doesn't love them more or you any less. He loves all of us the same because that's who He is, "For God is love" (1 John 4:3), and the sooner church leaders and hypocritical, self-righteous church folk understand that truth, the better off the church as a whole will be. Jesus addressed this very thing in Luke 18:9-14 Amplified Bible:

> "He also told this parable to some people who trusted in themselves and were confident that they were righteous [that they were upright and in right standing with God] and scorned and made nothing of all the rest of men: two men went up into the temple [enclosure] to pray, the one a Pharisee and the other a tax collector. The Pharisee took his stand ostentatiously and began to pray thus before and with himself: "God, I thank You that I am not like the rest of men—extortioners (robbers), swindlers (unrighteous heart and life), adulterers, or even like this tax collector here. I fast twice a week; I give tithes of all that I gain. But, the tax collector, [merely] standing at a distance, would not even lift up his eyes to Heaven, but kept striking his breast saying, "O God, be favorable [be gracious, be merciful] to me, the especially wicked sinner that I am"! I tell you, this man went down to his home justified (forgiven and made upright and in right standing with God), rather than the other man; "for everyone who exalts himself will be humbled, but he who humbles himself will be exalted."

Isn't that parable a description of some church folk you know or some church leaders you've heard? You know how they stick their chests out and their noses up, boasting about their fifteen-, twenty-, or thirty-year marriages—as if to say that because they've been married for that length of time, that gives them some special grace and places with God that divorced people aren't privy to. I say again, that's a bunch of crock! There is not one promise in the Bible that a divorced person does not have access to or can't get in position to have access to, not one.

Before we go on, let us clear the air about something. First, we're extremely pleased, happy, and excited to hear about long successful marriages. Praise God for them. Believe us, we have nothing at all against successful marriages, but we do have a bone of contention with the erroneous assumptions that those who have been blessed with successful marriages have; that divorced people enter into marriage with the intention of obtaining a divorce. Now, that's just plain stupid! I don't know of anyone who has entered into a marriage not wanting it to be their first and last one, but somewhere during the marriage, things change, people change, and things happen that shouldn't happen. There are a host of reasons why people end up divorced, but that doesn't make them any less of a person than those who have never divorced. If it weren't for God's great love in and through His Son Jesus, none of us would be worth anything. So those of you who are still in long blessed marriages, stop looking down your noses at divorced people, and especially you church leaders. Church leaders, do you realize how many new members and workers you would have if you got off of your holier than thou horses? Stop being part of the problem and become a part of the solution. Implement programs in your various churches that will reduce the number of divorces (i.e., how to trust God for a mate, being unequally yoked, the true meaning of love, how to keep Jesus first, disciplining the children and stepchildren, dividing labor in the home, and managing finances in the home, to name a few). But most of all, love them because a lot of people define God by the way leaders treat divorced people. "You are our epistle written in our hearts, *known and read by all men* (2 Corinthians 3:2) (emphasis mine). Leaders, do you truly understand that you have to give an account for all of the people that you've pushed away, rejected, and even hurt because of your erroneous view or mind-set regarding divorce? Whatever happened to the "whoever will let them come" doctrine? When did God start labeling and limiting folk from coming to Him?

Leaders, if you desire to be free from those erroneous mind-sets, agree as touching with us now: "Father, I come to you now in the name of Jesus and in the authority given to me in His name, I cast down every imagination, every theory, every confuting argument, every deceptive fantasy, every barrier of pride, every erroneous thought and I command them to flee and I command their thought life and mindsets to come under the authority of Christ and I release the ability for them to think on what's true, honest, just, pure, lovely, of good report and anything else that's of any virtue or anything deemed worthy of praise, in Jesus' name, amen."

Now, let us all walk in the love God has shed in our hearts by the Holy Spirit. Let our love light shine from the highest heights all over this world so that all people, including divorced people, can taste and see God's love.

> Herein is love, not that we loved God but that He loved us and sent His Son to be the propitiation for our sins. Beloved, if God so loved us, we ought also to love one another. No man has seen God at any time. If we love one another, God dwelleth in us and His love is perfected in us. (1 John 4:10-12)

> For the Father Himself loveth you. (John 16:27)

> For I am persuaded that neither death, nor life, nor angels, nor principalities, nor powers, nor things present, nor things to come, nor height, nor depth, nor any other creature shall be able to separate us from the love of God which is in Christ Jesus our Lord. (Romans 8:38-39)

Did you grasp that? There's nothing in existence, and there's nothing nonexistent that can prevent God from loving you, nothing, not even a divorce or divorces. So there you have it. The answer to the question, "Does God still love me?" Yes, yes, yes!

CHAPTER 3

Will God Forgive Me?

Will God forgive me is a question many ask themselves when they have gone through a divorce. They begin to doubt and question the very scriptures they need to find and use. For some strange reason, people think scriptures pertaining to forgiveness do not apply to divorced people, and I've never read in the Bible where God says, "My promises are for everybody in the world except divorced people. That's asinine, but it's the mentality of many people. They think divorce is the unpardonable sin, and for their ignorance, they give birth to more stupid assumptions. For instance, when people say or think you can't be forgiven from divorce, they're also saying Jesus died to every sin known and unknown to mankind except divorce. And the blood of Jesus is so powerful as to remove sin from generations past, generations present and generations to come, but when it comes to divorce, the blood loses its power. That's utterly ridiculous. 1 John 1:7 clearly shows us the blood of Jesus has the power to remove *all* sin, not all sin except divorce, but all sin.

Now, will God forgive you? Yes! But before we get to the scriptures that prove He has forgiven you, and will forgive you, I must share this important truth in respect to forgiveness. And that's Matthew 6:14-15, "For if you forgive men their trespasses, your heavenly Father will also forgive you. But if you do not forgive men their trespasses, neither will your Father forgive your trespasses." That's pretty clear. In order to receive forgiveness, you've first got to give forgiveness, which is a principle of sowing and reaping throughout the Bible and dealing with divorce. It's extremely difficult for some people to forgive their former mates, because after all, it's their fault they got divorced anyway. And that may very well be true. He or she may have done some horrendous things and you don't have to convince me of that.

In our society today, people are capable of doing some awful things to each other. "The heart is deceitful above all things, and desperately wicked" (Jeremiah 17:9). I understand that and now that you understand, it's time to move forward. And the first step is forgiving any and everybody that's wronged you or hurt you in any way. You may even be telling yourself I can't or won't ever forgive him/her or even them for that. But you must. When you harbor unforgiveness for anyone or anything, the one person you're hurting and harming the most is yourself. My brother or sister, hear me, if you're carrying any resentment, anger, hatred, unforgiveness, and the such like toward anyone, let it go.

Let's pray: "Father, help me to forgive _____ for all the pain, anger, resentment and hatred he/she/ they caused me. Your Word says You are my Helper and Deliverer. I, this day, cast all my care on You for You care for me and I ask You to keep me in Your peace, which passes all understanding, and release in me and through me, Your love and mercy. I, this day, have forgiven _____ from all he/she/they have done to me. Now, Father, let the power of Your forgiveness overtake me and cleanse me so that You can and will be glorified in me and through me in Jesus' name, amen."

Now we can proceed. Step two is forgiving yourself. Because you had a failed marriage doesn't make you a failure. Now that unforgiveness is gone, you now have established open access to the throne of God. He said, "Let us therefore come boldly to the throne of grace that we may obtain mercy and find grace to help in the time of need"

(Hebrews 4:16). So in learning to forgive yourself, spend plenty of time before the throne because it's there that you'll find all you need to assist you, comfort you, and direct you. All that you need, you're going to find at the throne; even the ability to stop blaming yourself. Yes, to stop blaming yourself. That's another mistake divorced people make, blaming themselves and building up walls of guilt and condemnation around themselves, and by doing that, they don't allow anyone into their world and they themselves become prisoners. Life again becomes difficult to deal with because you've blocked everyone out of your life, even God. When you block or keep God from helping you, you're destined to remain a prisoner in your walls of guilt and condemnation for as long as you choose to do so. "What do I do now?" some might ask. Well, the first thing to do is to invite God into the situation. He's always been there but you have the responsibility of inviting Him in. Remember Revelation 3:20, "Behold, I stand at the door and knock. If anyone … opens the door, I will come in." He's been standing at the door to many of our lives a long time. Don't you think it's time to open the door to your life and invite Him in? And when you invite Him in, He's going to tell you, "My precious, precious child, there's no condemnation now or forever to those who are in Christ Jesus." Then you're going to taste a deliverance and freedom like you've never experienced that's going to motivate you to search for more. The Holy Spirit will then show you other liberating scriptures pertaining to your complete forgiveness regarding guilt, condemnation, and divorce.

As I stated earlier, many people believe that divorce is the unpardonable sin and they go years, some to their graves, never receiving forgiveness for their divorce(s). But as we shall see in this chapter, "Will God forgive *me*?" He does forgive and He has forgiven you. First, let's deal with this fallacy that divorce is the unpardonable sin. Mark 3:28-30 (Amp) states, "Truly and solemnly I say to you, *all sins* will be forgiven the sons of men, and whatever abusive and blasphemous things they utter; But, whoever speaks abusively against or maliciously misrepresents the Holy Spirit can never get forgiveness, but is guilty of and in the grasp of an everlasting trespass. For they persisted in saying, He has an unclean spirit" (emphasis mine). Now where do you see divorce as the unpardonable sin in those verses? Nowhere!

For the sake of discussion or debate, let's reduce divorce down to its simplest form—sin. If you divorced for whatever, it's a sin. Stay with me now. Didn't Jesus Himself say in verse 28, "All sins will be forgiven." So what's the problem? My brother or sister, you've got to stop listening to man with his personal opinions concerning divorce and forgiveness. We're simply going to give you "The Word" so that you can come to your own conclusions. Will God forgive me? I say emphatically, "Yes!" And, here's my proof:

2 Corinthians 5:17 says, "Therefore, *if anyone* is in Christ Jesus, he is a new creation; old things have passed away; behold, all things have become new" (emphasis mine). I do believe that verse says "if anyone" and it doesn't say anyone except divorced people, does it?

Ephesians 1:7 states, "In Him we have redemption through His blood, the forgiveness of sins, according to the riches of His grace" (emphasis mine). What I want you to focus on is the first two words of that verse—"In Him." For it is in Jesus, through Jesus and because of Jesus that we have access to forgiveness. No man or men, I don't care who they are or how many there are, can prevent Jesus from extending His forgiveness to you. He's made forgiveness available to you. Now it's up to you to receive and accept it. The second thing I want you to bring to your attention is the four words "the forgiveness of sins." It would have been just fine to just say "the forgiveness," which would imply that we all could be forgiven, but the scripture didn't stop there. It went on to say "forgiveness of sins," which tells us that God wanted to make it perfectly clear that not only will you be forgiven when you accept Jesus as your personal Lord and Savior, but all of your sins will be blotted out as though they never happened—and now that you are a part of God's family, you have access to forgiveness, always. There's one more thing I'd like to point out, and that's when the scripture says, "Through His blood, the forgiveness of sins." Notice that it's by the power of the blood of Jesus that we have forgiveness of our sins and not by the permission or choice of man. Also notice that it doesn't say divorce is the only sin that the blood of Jesus doesn't have the ability to forgive—*no!* The scripture says, "In Him we have redemption through His blood, the forgiveness of sins," and that would and does include forgiveness for divorce(s).

I believe the case has been made that God does forgive divorced people, but we're going to give you a few more scriptures to solidify our case.

I John 1:9 states, "If we confess our sins, He is faithful and just to forgive us our sins, and to cleanse us from all unrighteousness." Notice our responsibility; we must confess our sins, and that includes divorces. So when we go to God honestly, sincerely, and humbly and tell Him we missed it, we messed up, we made a mistake or whatever way you're led to tell Him, He's bound by His love and His Word to forgive you. And God doesn't stop with forgiveness. He goes on to cleanse you. If you will allow Him to, He will cleanse all the bitterness, hatred, failure, low self-esteem, and whatever else is attempting to hinder you. Another important point we must make in this verse is that the focus must be on God—"If we confess our sins to God, He is faithful and just to forgive us" (1 John 1:9). God will forgive, but man, on the other hand, will try to use your divorce against you, continually bringing it up to you but thank God for being God. It is He that matters. As long as God forgives you, you're forgiven and regardless of what man may think of you. There's nothing man can do to hinder or hurt your relationship with God. And after God forgives your sin(s), look at what else He does: "For I will be merciful to their unrighteousness and their sin(s) and iniquities will I remember no more" (Hebrews 8:12). What an awesome promise from God. Not only does God forgive us, but as far as God is concerned, it's as though it never happened. You can understand the first part of Numbers 23:19, "God is not a man."

More clearly now, God not only forgives us, He refuses to remember our sin(s) again. The New Testament: A translation in the language of the people (Charles B. Williams) says it like this, "And never, never anymore will I recall their sins." (Thank God that He alone is God!) Man, on the other hand, will not only refuse to forget your mistakes, failures, and shortcomings, but at every opportunity they get, they will throw it up in your face and to whomever else will listen to them. Now you can expect the world and unsaved folk to behave like that, but church folk, saved folk, and Holy Ghost-filled folk aren't supposed to conduct themselves like that. They're not *supposed* to conduct themselves like that, but the sad reality of it is that they will talk about you and spread your business faster than worldly unsaved folk! The scriptures very clearly teach us that we're to be imitators of God as dear children (Ephesians 5:1). As children attempt to copy their earthly parents, we're supposed to copy our Heavenly Father. Here are a few things that we're supposed to do: "Be ye therefore merciful as your Father also is merciful" (Luke 6:36) and "And be kind one to another, tenderhearted, forgiving one another, even as God in Christ forgave you" (Ephesians 4:32).

Now tell me, are those characteristics of God present in the body of Christ or even your local church? Therein lies the problem with divorced people. They've for too long identified or classified themselves based on the perceptions of hypocritical church folk. It's our desire to allow divorced people to see themselves through the eyes of God's love and to elevate their sights from man to God. The scriptures tell us "looking unto Jesus," and as you do that, I promise you that you will begin to see and experience some major changes in your life. So once again, I say stop listening and believing all of the negativity that comes from man and as God told the disciples on the Mount of Transfiguration—*hear Him*!

CHAPTER 4

Will God Still Use Me?

People often think that because they're divorced, they're no good to God anymore. Unfortunately, a lot of those misconceptions have come from behind the pulpits of our churches.

It amazes me how people perpetuate lies in the church, especially concerning divorce. I've discovered, through the teaching of the Holy Spirit, that the majority of the messages presented pertaining to divorce are inaccurate and extremely opinionated. Jesus never told us that our opinions have the power to do anything for us. He did say, "If you abide in my Word, you are my disciples indeed. And, you shall know the truth and the truth will make you free" (John 8:31-32). Only when we hear the truth and develop a relationship with the truth can the truth be allowed to unleash its power to liberate us. That's one of the primary reasons why many divorced people haven't endeavored to fulfill their God-given assignment—a lack of truth.

"Will God still use me?" is a question many divorced people have pondered over and over. Now we're going to answer that question, not with opinions but with the Word of the Living God. Romans 11:29 says, "For the gifts and calling of God are irrevocable." So what does "irrevocable" mean? According to *Webster's New World*

DIVORCE: THROUGH THE EYES OF GOD'S LOVE

Dictionary, Second College Edition, it means that something cannot be revoked, recalled, or undone. In other words, whatever God has called or equipped you to do before your divorce, He expects you to carry it out or fulfill it after your divorce (Those are praise giving words—Hallelujah!). God will never revoke or recall your gift because of divorce. Man may demote you, remove you and not use you, but God is not man.

Because of our ignorance and lack of truth on the subject of divorce, many divorced people are allowing their gifts to lie dormant within them and because they're not using their gifts, they think God is angry at them or has taken back their gift(s). Don't you know that before you were divorced, God knew you would be divorced and He still called you and placed a gift or gifts in you? Jeremiah 1:4-5 says, "Then the Word of the Lord came to me, saying: Before I formed you in the womb, I knew you; Before you were born, I sanctified you." Now, that's not restricted to Jeremiah. It applies to all of us. Before we were formed in our mother's womb, God knew us. So, if He knew us before we knew ourselves and still chose to call us and use us, why would he stop using us after a divorce? One of God's attributes is that He's omniscient, meaning He knows *all*. So again, if God already knew you before you knew yourself, and God knew you were going to get a divorce even before you were ever married, and He still chose to call you and use you, what's your problem? *Stop* listening to man and *start* listening to God.

Will God still use you? The answer is yes. But again, why not let God answer for Himself:

> At THAT TIME JESUS COMETH TO a city of Samaria, which is called Sychar, near to the parcel of ground that Jacob gave to his son Joseph. Now Jacob's well was there. Jesus therefore, being wearied with his journey, sat thus on the well: and it was about the sixth hour. There cometh a woman of Samaria to draw water: Jesus saith unto her, Give me to drink. (For his disciples were gone away unto

the city to buy meat.) Then saith the woman of Samaria unto him, How is it that thou, being a Jew, askest drink of me, which am a woman of Samaria? for the Jews have no dealings with the Samaritans. Jesus answered and said unto her, If thou knewest the gift of God, and who it is that saith to thee, Give me to drink; thou wouldest have asked of him, and he would have given thee living water. The woman saith unto him, Sir, thou hast nothing to draw with, and the well is deep: from whence then hast thou that living water? Art thou greater than our father Jacob, which gave us the well, and drank thereof himself, and his children, and his cattle? Jesus answered and said unto her, Whosoever drinketh of this water shall thirst again: But whosoever drinketh of the water that I shall give him shall never thirst; but the water that I shall give him shall be in him a well of water springing up into everlasting life. The woman saith unto him, Sir, give me this water, that I thirst not, neither come hither to draw. Jesus saith unto her, Go, call thy husband, and come hither. The woman answered and said, I have no husband. Jesus said unto her, Thou hast well said, I have no husband: For thou hast had five husbands; and he whom thou now hast is not thy husband: in that saidst thou truly. The woman saith unto him, Sir, I perceive that thou art a prophet. Our fathers worshipped in this mountain; and ye say, that in Jerusalem is the place where men ought to worship. Jesus saith unto her, Woman, believe me, the hour cometh, when ye shall neither in this mountain, nor yet at Jerusalem, worship the Father. Ye worship ye know not what: we know what we worship: for salvation is of the Jews. But the hour cometh, and now is, when the true worshippers shall worship the Father in spirit and in truth: for the Father seeketh such to worship him. God is a Spirit: and they that worship him must worship him in spirit and in truth. The woman saith unto him, I know that Messias cometh, which is called Christ: when he is come, he will tell us all things. Jesus saith unto her, I that speak unto thee am he. And upon this came his disciples, and marvelled that he talked with the woman: yet no man said, What seekest thou? or, Why talkest thou with her? The woman then left her waterpot, and went her way into the city, and saith to the men, Come, see a man, which told me all things that ever I did: is not this the Christ? Then they went out of the city, and came unto him. In the mean while his disciples prayed him, saying, Master, eat. But he said unto them, I have meat to eat that ye know not of. Therefore said the disciples one to another, Hath any man brought him ought to eat? Jesus saith unto them, My meat is to do the will of him that sent me, and to finish his work. Say not ye, There are yet four months, and then cometh harvest? behold, I say unto you, Lift up your eyes, and look on the fields; for they are white already to harvest. And he that reapeth receiveth wages, and gathereth fruit unto life eternal: that both he that soweth and he that reapeth may rejoice together. And herein is that saying true, One soweth, and another reapeth. I sent you to reap that whereon ye bestowed no labour: other men laboured, and ye are entered into their labours. And many of the Samaritans of that city believed on him for the saying of the woman, which testified, He told me all that ever I did. So when the Samaritans were come unto him, they besought him that he would tarry with them: and he abode there two days. And many more believed because of his own word; And said unto the woman, Now we believe, not because of thy saying: for we have heard him ourselves, and know that this is indeed the Christ, the Saviour of the world. (John 4:4-42)

There was a certain Samaritan woman who came to draw water and ended up meeting the One who made the water. Let's see what God tells us through her.

First, Jesus dialogued with a divorced woman. Yes, Jesus, Emmanuel, which being interpreted is "God with us." So God talked with, conversed with, and had a discussion with a divorced person. Isn't that amazing? Jesus sat down (verse 6) and gave this divorced person His undivided attention and allowed her to actually talk to Him (*God in the flesh!*). But church folk won't allow a divorced person to talk to them without a condescending or judgmental attitude. Who's greater, God or man? If God is willing to listen to divorced people, then what in the world is church folk, especially church leaders, problem?

Secondly, Jesus revealed something to her (a divorced person that He explicitly told the disciples not to tell anyone. In Matthew 16:13-20, Jesus asked the question, "Who do men say that I Am?" After the other disciples' response, Simon Peter was the only one who responded correctly by saying that Jesus was the Christ, the Son of the Living God. And Jesus went on to tell Simon Peter that he was blessed and that flesh and blood did not reveal that to him, but His Father in heaven. Now, let's look at verse 20, "Then He commanded His disciples that they should *tell no one* that He was Jesus the Christ" (emphasis mine). Now why would Jesus command His disciples not to make known something and then He Himself revealed it to a divorced person? Remember Matthew 16:20, "Then He commanded His disciples that they should *tell no one* that He was Jesus the Christ" (emphasis mine). Now let us look at John 4:25-26, "The woman said to Him, I know that Messiah is coming [Who is called Christ]. When He comes, He will tell us all things. Jesus said to her, I Who speak to you Am He [good God ALMIGHTY!]." Jesus revealed something to this divorced person that He forbade His disciples to share. "Why?" some are wondering. Well, *one* of the reasons, I believe, is to show this woman, and not only this divorced person, but to show every divorced person through the ages, that despite what man may say to you or about you, you're still special and important to Him. Though society looks down their noses at you, church folk overlook you and church leaders prevent you from being used, Jesus is showing us through this revelation of Himself that even though this woman was divorced, He didn't want her to receive this revelation from anyone other than Himself. Divorced people, please hear what the Spirit is saying. He's letting us know, "Though you may be divorced from man, you're already one with Him." He'll never leave you or forsake you. Also, as Jesus revealed Himself as the Christ to this divorced person, there are many things that He desires to reveal to you. He desires to reveal to you an abundance of peace and truth (Jeremiah 33:6). But you've got to stop listening to all the negativity from man and grasp (hold onto) whatever it was or is that God spoke to you.

Lastly (and you may want to buckle your seat belt on this one), "Will God still use me?" Yes! Here we have a woman who's been divorced five times—yes, five times—and yet Jesus allows her to utilize her Evangelist gift. John 4:28-30 and 39-42, state, "*The woman* then *left her water-pot, went her way into the city and said to the men, Come, see a man Who told me all things that I ever did*" (emphasis mine). Could this be the Christ? Then "*they went out of the city and came to Him. And many of the Samaritans of that city believed in Him because of the word of the woman*" (emphasis mine) who testified, "He told me all that I ever did. So when the Samaritans had come to Him, they urged Him to stay with them. And He stayed there two more days. And many more believed because of His own Word. Then they said to the woman, "Now we believe, not because of what you said, for we ourselves have heard Him and we know that this is indeed the Christ, the Savior of the world [good God ALMIGHTY!]." Here we have indisputable, unquestionable, and indissoluble proof that God will use a divorced person! Did you notice that Jesus didn't stop her and say, "You can't evangelize a city or witness for me because you've been divorced?" Neither did He tell her that because of her divorce, He couldn't use her or that she's no use to Him because of her divorce. No! Jesus welcomed her gift, and *many* were won to Him because of her. Ask all of those self-righteous, hypocritical church folk and church leaders, "How many people in *their* city have *they* won to Christ?"

My dear brother or sister in Christ, one of the most important lessons I've ever learned and a lesson you too must learn is to stop allowing man to limit you, label you, and restrict you. God loved you before the divorce, He loves you after the divorce, and He will always love you. You're very special to God. Psalm 17:8 says, "You're the *apple* of God's eye" (emphasis mine). So don't allow anybody to tell you anything different.

CHAPTER 5

What about the Children?

One of the most overlooked areas during a divorce is the children. We oftentimes take their emotional status for granted. If your child or children are at an age where you can sit them down and discuss your decision to obtain a divorce, I believe you should do so. Because you always want them to feel loved and appreciated, when we neglect to inform them about divorce, children tend to feel isolated and responsible for the breakup, especially after a divorce when one of the parents stops visiting the child (We'll discuss this in more detail later). When having children, one of the most important truths you need never forget is Psalm 127:3, which states, "Lo, children are an heritage of the Lord: and the fruit of the womb is His reward." Other translations make reference to the fact that children are gifts from God to us. And so since children are gifts from God, shouldn't we love, cherish, protect, and provide for them? Yes. And part of your loving is being honest and open with them about your divorce. You don't ever want them to hear the reasons for your divorce from outside sources. Because you very well know how folk tend to exaggerate, speculate, and gravitate toward negativity. Too often, children are told the wrong things, and those wrong things can cripple a child's growth in a number of ways. Again, that's why it is so important for the parent or parents of the child(ren) to sit them down and explain as clear as possible and be as specific as possible about the reasons for the dissolution of your marriage. And as you do so, constantly affirm your love for them. Because children need to be assured that your decision to divorce is not their fault as they need to be assured that they will continue to be loved by *both parents*.

A very tragic mistake the noncustodial parent(s) make is disappearing from the lives of the children. Some of these parents don't even have the decency to provide for these children financially. I believe that is one of the world's greatest sins to totally abandon and neglect innocent children. As parents, we have a God given responsibility to our children, first to love them. In Titus 2:2-4, we're taught to be sound in love and to love our children. Secondly, we're taught to provide for them. 1 Timothy 5:8 says, "But if any provide not for his own, and specially for those of his own house, he hath denied the faith, and is worse than an infidel." Can the scriptures get any clearer than that? *Parents have a God-given responsibility to provide for their children,* and it doesn't end because you've gotten a divorce. I don't understand how some parents can assume that because they're divorced from their spouse, they're divorced from their parental responsibilities as well. That's got to be one of the most asinine assumptions ever: to think that because you're divorced, you don't have to provide for your children. Those are *your* children, not the states'. As a matter of fact, they don't belong to the grandparents, either. What a sad trend that has developed over the years. Grandparents can't enjoy the freedom of their last years on earth. They can't travel, visit, or spend their own money on what they want because they're shackled to their children's children. It doesn't appear that the children are grateful or appreciative of all the sacrifices that Dad and Mom or Dad or Mom for them coming up, and now they want to push their responsibilities off on them again. Now, I'm not saying that grandparents shouldn't spend time with their grandchildren because I believe most grandparents love their grandchildren and love it when their grandchildren *visit*. But when it comes to keeping them for extended periods of time, don't assume that grandparents want to do that. Grandparents are in a different frame of mind now. When they were parents, their mind-set was parental, which is different when the children were their primary responsibility, their own children. But now after all the sacrificing and putting their lives on hold in a lot of areas and seeing to it that their own children had food, clothing, a roof over their head and got an education, it is now time for them to enjoy themselves but now their children are being selfish, uncaring and irresponsible by asking them to take on the responsibility of raising their grandchildren. I ask you, "Is that fair?" We should cherish our parents. The Bible says, "Honor thy father and thy mother." And how many of you understand that's a lifelong commandment. Even when parents become grandparents, we're to honor and respect them and not try to take advantage of them. We should not only *allow* them to enjoy the remainder of their days but *help* them to enjoy the remainder of their days.

Parents, our children are our responsibility to raise, provide for, love, discipline, guide, and protect. We are the ones responsible for their being here, so stop getting angry with the world and whoever else you're aiming your anger at. If, for whatever reason, you might need some assistance with your child or children, the first thing you need to do is pray and ask God for help. He says in Philippians 4:6 not to worry about anything but tell Him every detail of your needs in earnest and thankful prayer. And when we do things God's way, things happen the right way. He may have all types of people and agencies volunteering to help you. But we must do things the right way, especially when it comes to our children.

CHAPTER 6

What's Worst?

In this chapter, we're simply going to look at the lives of some of our great biblical leaders and see some of the mistakes, failures, and sins that were a part of their lives. So as to broaden our perspective to the act of divorce, folks tend to want to put divorced people at the bottom of the list and make them the worst of the worst. Even though the scriptures say, "All unrighteousness is sin" (1 John 5:17), we're going to do a comparative analysis with the lives of these great leaders and you tell us "what's worse?"

- Let's begin with *Abraham* in Genesis 20. We have an account of Abraham *lying* to Abimelech about Sarah, his wife, and according to verse 13, Abraham convinced his own wife to join him in telling the lie. Here it is, a man God Himself establishes a covenant with, out of *fear*, refuses to tell folk that Sarah is indeed his wife. So we have here a lying, fearful Abraham who's putting the lives of innocent people in jeopardy. Had it not been for the grace of God to intervene because of His covenant with Abraham, a lot of innocent people would have died. So what's worse? A lying, fearful person who jeopardizes the lives of others or an honest and bold divorced person?

- Now let's take a look at Noah, Genesis 9:21 and 24a: "And he drank of the wine, and was drunken; and he was uncovered within his tent. And Noah awoke from his wine." Noah was what we call "sloppy drunk." The man got so drunk that he took all of his clothes off (got buck-naked). Not only that, he was so intoxicated that he passed out and had to sleep it off. To our religious folk, I guess that's acceptable. It's all right to be a drunk. Just don't be divorced. Again, I ask you, what's worse? A buck-naked drunk or a sober divorced person? It amazes me how folk attempt to classify faults, failures and sin. I pray God delivers us all from it because that brings us to the place that James warns us about, "Are ye not then partial in yourselves and are become judges of evil thoughts" (verse 4). Another way to say that is this: "Are you not discriminating among your own and becoming prejudiced judges?"
- Next we have *Peter*, probably the most known apostle/disciple. In Luke 22:56-61, he denies that he knows or even associates with Jesus. How can this man, who has been with Jesus practically the entire time of Jesus' ministry, witnessed innumerable miracle healings, deliverances, even heard God Himself make reference to Jesus on the Mount of Transfiguration. How can he deny Jesus three times? Yes, three times! Moments earlier in verse 33, he'd just finished telling Jesus, "I am ready to go with thee, both into prison, and to death." Then he let a girl scare him into denying Jesus (verse 56). But again, our religious hypocrites can embrace Peter's denial of the Master three times, lying in Jesus's face, telling Him that he's going to be with Him, if need be, in prison and even death, then letting a girl scare him. But let someone announce that they've been through a divorce. I suppose in the eyes of church folk, a divorce is much worse than denying Jesus.
- Now we have the man responsible for the first five books of the Bible, *Moses*. Did you know that according to Exodus 2:11-15, *Moses was a murderer*? The Bible tells us that he

went out to see the "hard life," the heavy labor his brethren, the Hebrews, had to endure and when he noticed one of the Egyptians hitting a fellow Hebrew, Moses didn't like it. So Moses killed the Egyptian and buried him in the sand. Now, nowhere in this chapter or the preceding chapter do we find God instructing Moses to kill someone. But he did and because he killed an Egyptian, the Pharaoh wanted to kill Moses. The point is this: if the religious world can embrace a murderer, why can't they find it in their hypocritical hearts to forgive and embrace a divorced person?

- Next up, we have *David*. Yes, King David. In 2 Samuel 11, we have David as a Peeping Tom, knowingly committing adultery with Bathsheba. Not only that, he had the woman's husband, Uriah, killed and then marries the lady. You say, "The nasty, lowdown, dirty dog!" The great King David wasn't a perfect, faultless king, was he? This anointed king who defeated Goliath, who was a gifted musician, who was responsible for writing a great number of the Psalms, and being especially known for the Twenty-Third Psalm, this man who is probably quoted every Sunday. Isn't that something to think about? Here it is. We can stand up in our pulpits and admire, adore, applause, and accept a Peeping Tom and murderer, yet from the same pulpit, look down our noses with such contempt at divorced people. What's worse? A Peeping Tom, wife-stealing murderer or a God-fearing divorced person?
- Finally, we have *Paul*, formerly known as Saul. The Apostle Paul of the tribe of Benjamin, educated in Jerusalem in the School of Gamaliel, a Pharisee and responsible for writing about half of the New Testament. This man persecuted Christians, consented to the stoning death of Stephen, and went so far as to enter the homes of Christians and drag them out, both men and women (Acts). Paul gave Christians a taste of hell. Yes, the great Apostle Paul. Can you imagine the nerve of Paul persecuting God's children, standing and watching as they stoned Stephen as Stephen called out to

God and talked to Jesus. But the amazing thing about Paul is that after he persecuted God's children, God forgave him and used him mightily. Now, if God can forgive Paul and use him to bless His people, why can't or why won't church folk and church leaders forgive divorced people and allow their gifts to be a blessing to them and to others?

We, as the body of Christ, must begin to conduct ourselves like the head of the body. He wasn't hypocritical in His views about people. Jesus loved everyone. He didn't place liars above thieves, Pharisees above publicans, and adulterers above tax-collectors. No! Jesus loved them all and died for them all. But for some strange reason, church folk think one sinner is worse than another and in doing that, we create prejudicial, warped, and superficial churches.

When are we going to obey this new commandment that Jesus gave to us? John 13:34 says, "A new commandment I give unto you, that you love one another; as I have loved you that you also love one another." He didn't say to judge one another, classify one another according to one's sins. No! Jesus said for us to love one another as He loves us. So it shouldn't matter if brother or sister so and so has been divorced. We are commanded to love them. When you refuse to love or accept a divorced person, remember, you're not just rejecting the divorced person—you're also rejecting and violating God's love law. So what's worse? Loving and embracing a divorced person or rejecting and violating God's love law?

CHAPTER 7

Can I Remarry?

Deuteronomy 24:1-4 states, "When a man takes a wife and marries her, and it happens that she finds no favor in his eyes because he has found some uncleanness in her, and he writes her a certificate of divorce, puts it in her hand, and sends her out of his house, when she has departed from his house, and *goes and becomes another man's wife*, if the latter husband detests her and writes her a certificate of divorce, puts it in her hand and sends her out of his house, or if the latter husband dies who took her as his wife, then her former husband who divorced her must not take her back to be his wife after she has been defiled" (emphasis mine).

In these verses, the scriptures imply that this woman could be married at least three times and that's without fornication being involved. I mentioned fornication specifically for the sake of those hard-hearted church folk who attempt to bind folk to the idea that the only grounds you have for obtaining a divorce is fornication. Yes, Jesus did say, "It hath been said, Whoever shall put away his wife, let him give her a writing of divorcement: But I say unto you, that whosoever shall put away his wife, saving for the cause of fornication, causeth her to commit adultery: and, whosoever shall marry her that is divorced committeth adultery" (Matthew 5:31-32). In the eyes of some church folk, that's crystal clear, but what you really have with a lot of church folk is "the blind leading the blind." They have not yet become able or competent ministers of our New Covenant. They wish to hold us to the letter of the law not understanding how the Spirit gives life.

Even though Jesus said, "It hath been said, Whoever shall put away his wife, let him give her a writing of divorcement: But I say unto you, that whosoever shall put away his wife, saving for the cause of fornication, causeth her to commit adultery: and, whosoever shall marry her that is divorced committeth adultery" (Matthew 5:31-32). And elsewhere in the scriptures, Jesus stated it was God's intent from the beginning that when a man and a woman leave father and mother they should cleave to each other, becoming one flesh. That was God's intent, but when Adam sinned, he opened the door for mankind to do a whole lot of things outside of God's original plan. Let us say this, it is still God's desire for us to marry (man and woman) and stay married until death, but ever since sin entered our world, that has not been the case. God's showing his great love for us, instituted many new laws to reveal not only His love but also His mercy. Quite naturally, whenever Jesus teaches us, it's always God's best or His setting the highest standards for us. I believe one of the areas we misunderstand in respect to divorce is "there is fixed laws or truths and there are exceptions to some laws and truths." Now, in respect to divorce, it can't be a fixed law whereby the only way one can get a divorce is "if fornication has occurred." Because there are other scriptures that allow divorce without fornication:

- Deuteronomy 24:1-4 says, "A husband can divorce his wife *if she finds no favor* in his eyes" (emphasis mine). It also says, "If the second husband *comes to hate her, he too can divorce her*" (emphasis mine).
- 1 Corinthians 7:10-15 shows us that if our mates are unsaved or unbelievers and they depart or divorce us, we're free.

Now, nowhere in these scriptures do you see the reason for or leading to divorce was fornication. Let us say again, we do believe it's God desire for us to marry once, until death do us part, but if that's not your situation, don't allow anybody to keep you from remarrying. You can remarry! 1 Corinthians 7:27-28 says, "Art thou loosed from a wife? Seek not to be loosed. Art thou loosed from a wife? Seek not a wife. *But and if thou marry, thou hast not sinned*" (emphasis mine). That tells me that if you're married, try to stay married, and if you're divorced, don't rush into another marriage. But if you choose to remarry, you haven't sinned!

The choice is yours. You can continue to allow ignorant folk to make your life miserable by telling you that you can't or shouldn't remarry or you can take God at His Word, knowing He's going to love you whether you choose to remarry or stay single.

But yes! You can remarry!

For more information regarding the author or speaking engagements or additional copies of this booklet contact:

>John Allen, Jr.
>P.O. Box 554
>Ocoee, FL 34761
>407-883-8965
>Fax:
>E-mail: jallenjr@aol.com

ABOUT THE AUTHOR

I'm extremely humbled and grateful to be one of God's children. I'm married to a beautiful woman inside and out Mrs. Erica Allen. I'm the father of La Shawnta, Harmony, John III, Victoria, and Diamond. I have a master's degree in theological studies and is currently being used to oversee Communion Ministries International, Inc. I'm also a man given to much prayer, much thanks to Jesus my Lord, and much dependence on the Holy Spirit.

CPSIA information can be obtained
at www.ICGtesting.com
Printed in the USA
LVHW090044120319
610321LV00001B/37/P